SPIRIT CABINET

PITT POETRY SERIES

Ed Ochester, Editor

David Wojahn

SPIRIT CABINET

UNIVERSITY OF PITTSBURGH PRESS

FOR NOELLE WATSON

 The publication of this book is supported by a grant from the Pennsylvania Council on the Arts

Published by the University of Pittsburgh Press, Pittsburgh, Pa., 15260
Copyright © 2002, David Wojahn
Manufactured in the United States of America
Printed on acid-free paper
10 9 8 7 6 5 4 3 2 1

ISBN 0-8229-5776-0

One evening in Port Glasgow, when unable to write due to a jazz band playing in the drawing room just below me, I walked up along the road past the gas works to where I saw a cemetery on a gently rising slope.... I seemed then to see that it rose in the midst of a great plain, and that all in the plain were resurrecting and moving towards it.... I knew then that the Resurrection would be directed from this hill.... Resurrection through a harmony between the quick and the dead, between the visitors to a cemetery and the dead now rising from it.... I had the feeling that each grave forms a part of a person's home just as their front gardens do, so that a row of graves and a row of cottage gardens have much the same meaning to me.

STANLEY SPENCER

Contents

III

IV

I

To Hermes Are Attributed Three Inventions: Music, Writing, Fire

One day old he raised himself from his crib
to kill a tortoise inching past, & on the second day

he ventured forth to steal & slay the fatted sacred
cattle of Apollo his brother, some to offer up

in sacrifice to Zeus, others to gut & string
their innards along the tortoise shell,

thereby inventing the lyre, & from the lyre
music. Let it be attested, then, that song arises from

the punished flesh: the finch more sweetly warbles
after the white-hot wires have pierced its eyes.

Thus Mandelstam at Voronezh, who staggers
in his dogskin coat on plankboard streets

while children taunt him, not quite dead
but surely mad, not yet swaddled by the permafrost

& gulag razor wire, but caged so fully within himself
that only the dense clandestine singing

issues forth. *Don't make comparisons*
he wrote, *the living are incomparable.*

But of the dead what shall persist?
What plucked notes in a tongue I cannot read,

what stanzas where he's alloyed to
the finch's keening, perched inside the strict

& molten wire, cuttlebone & flutter & trapeze,
trill of the feral notes ascending & the head thrown back?

The head thrown back & thus not vanishing,
though the cattle car doors shall still slide open

in the transit camps, & on a smoldering garbage heap
he'll last be seen to climb, sifting

empty cans for scraps of food. & this too
is incomparable. O Cunning One,

Swift Pilot of the wingéd sandals, whose
helmet gleams of burnished gold,

O Master of aeries & patron of thieves,
of the roseate horizon & empurpled cloud,

look down now upon Thy makings.
Behold what Thy hands have done.

Cartouche

(Valley of the Kings, 1997)

First, destroy the face. The hands
  & sandaled feet—blunt them as well.
& within the ochre-daubed cartouche,

 chisel to smithereens the great floating eye
  of Horus. Now the living God within the stone
 walks hobbled. Erect instead Thy own cartouche

  so that Thou as well shall incarnate the God:

thus did Thutmose III erase his aunt Queen
  Hatshepsut from every wall & pillar of her temple,
 from glyph-encrusted stairs & porticos, alcoves,

 chambers, capitals. Now the desecrating
  God-eye scans us all. Someone to watch. Now the tourist
 police in mufti smoke beneath the friezed colonnades,

  AK-47s & their bayonets agleam, while in the ticket

booth the radio's on scan—Cairo talk show,
  BBC & muezzin's wail, finally alighting
 on "Hotel California" ("Such a lonely place. . . . ").

 The Polish archaeologists inch rope ladders
  to their excavation, jackhammers & box lunches
 creaking down on pulleys, while N. zigzags

  the Grand Staircase, her Nikon clicking, shades

& flapper straw hat. The rest of us in shadow
        sip canteens, jackal-faced Anubis glaring down;
Hatshepsut's expedition to the Land of Punt,

    chiseled triremes, the galleys' billowed sails,
        & forty-seven bearers, baskets laden—myrrh & monkey-hides,
azure paint visible still. Someone to watch,

        someone to watch the watchers—say from the foothills

above, binoculars trained on N., on Hesham our guide.
        Looking up, we might have glimpsed the sun
(107 Fahrenheit) flare against their lenses

    & bandoliers. But when the Koran scholars
        finally charge, having cased the temple site
for seven months, streaming to the courtyard with

        machine guns stuttering, killing fifty-four tourists,

mostly Italian and Dutch, six Polish archaeologists,
        & martyring of course themselves,
we will have been home for weeks. Someone to watch:

    lenses' crosshairs trained on N., her sunscreen-slathered
        neck & shoulders, which unto dawn I have caressed.
Last night on the terrace of the Luxor Hilton,

        David regaled us with stories, government work,

"the Agency," before retiring to travel. Saigon,
        Congo, Bolivia stalking Che. His more
sober wife trying vainly to cut him off.

His first job after law school: subaltern
        for the Warren Commission. One morning
all the Congressmen & functionaries

        gathered in a basement screening room

to watch Zapruder nineteen times. The screen
        going blank as the reel coughed off, rewound
& commenced again, Marlboros & cigars

        aglow to ghost the screen, pink pillbox
        hat of Jackie, hands cradling
the precious rubied brain, then cradling again.

        Again projector whirr & fidget,

matches lit, again the jitter of pens on legal pads,
        blood-flare of the cranium (someone to watch . . .)
again. David taps the tabletop, finishing his gimlet.

        Next day, same thing, & the next & the next.
        All that summer (rewind, chisel) do you see
my point? Silence now, glint of N.'s earring

        & the blue vein throbbing her neck. The yellow

strings of patio lights lean down,
        reflections blinking on the turbid Nile.
Is this what I now look upon?

        Or is it N. strolling to me in the chiaroscuroed
        shadow of the hypostyle hall,
pulse of her flash against the pillars? Someone shouts

        in Polish. Then the hammer's percussive cry.

To the Memory of Paul Celan

i.
The Sea Captain's Gift, 1654

The whale's rheumy eye is brandy-pickled; its jar
sucks in the light, bobbing huge as a baby's head,

hairless and glistening, aswim in coppery liquid,
the briny swirl, the lidless unblinking stare,

sinew and blubbery fringe
                              where the saws and axes
extracted it from Greenland shoals,

from scaffold and tryworks, vats of tallow
bubbling in the night-long twilight of arctic

July. The gracious Captain Hoekensteck
removes his hat and bows to
                              Doctor Leeuwenhoek,

astronomer and alchemist, inventor of the microscope,
who beside his astrolabs and beakers will dissect

Leviathan's optic nerve.
                              Vermeer portrays him in a robe
of Cathay silk. His hand spins a backlit, cartouched globe.

ii.
Twins, Blue Tears, 1943

Blue dye aswirl in the Jew-twin's eyes,
procaine on the needle-tip to dull the pain,

cerulean liquid in slow spasms from his syringe,
lid propped open, needle on the white—
                                        then the cry

from both twins' throats, "though only *one*
receives the dye today. *Intriguing!* She trembles

when her sister trembles. . . . "
                        And Doctor Mengele
makes note of this, fumbles in his labcoat for a bon-bon.

A little gift. Blue tears river the girl's face.
A gift. Her sister watches the shaved head thrash,

then slowly calm, gentling to Mengele's touch.
"The Aryanization proceeds apace. . . ."

A magnifying glass:
                        he smiles as the mixture spirals
blue and white, like oceans in satellite photos.

iii.
A Visit to Port Arthur, 1995

Where the soul is 13,000 miles from home.
But where is home?
                     All the tour buses in Tasmania

are parked outside the penal colony ruins.
The rehabbed madhouse holds us prisoner

to posters, t-shirts, Pepsi and *The Fatal Shore,*
and the cell doors of the Model Prison open

to the light meters' probe.
                  O soul the red lights flicker,
announcing the flashbulbs' lockdown.

Here the hooded nameless *convict's convicts* came,
gentled o soul by the cat and triangles,

the coffin cells, regressing them down to the womb's
original sinlessness,
                  reborn wet and fetal,

yanked into a light as strange and speechless
as aphasia.
        O Soul black milk thy lamentation endless.

Symposium

The little cage rocks forward. The albino rears up hissing.
  You can see the rows of teats, engorged & seeping
    milk against the mesh. A trail of carrion,

of marshmallows doctored with bacon grease
  has lead us to this howl & clamor in the rain-drenched
    yard. The count this morning's three: two pups

shrieking in the smaller cage, while the white-faced
  possum mother shoots her blood-flecked paw at them,
    also shrieking, chorus as grating as Chinese opera.

How many dwell there under us, scurrying the porch
  & basement ceiling tiles, spelunking crawl space
    to scoop with their practiced delicacy the eyes

& tongues of sparrows, cellophane impearled with chicken fat,
  rosettes of beef blood, orange peel freckled
    with coffee grounds & sweetly fetid? *Trapper John*

Incorporated's set the snares: Trapper & his girlfriend
  more precisely. Double majors, wildlife management
    & MBA, they once bagged twenty from a house

down the block. But they're in class this morning:
  nothing to do now but wait. Hospital ruins, mud-filled
    craters on Serb TV, & from Belgrade a "Minister

without Portfolio" announces the refugees are actors,
  all of them on NATO's payroll. Cover the cages
    & the shrieks might die. So with yard gloves & a sheet

I matador a path toward her: we've been warned
    about the claws. Wildly they slither the mesh.
        Salmon-pink, her eyes are fixed on me.

In the naked bed, in Plato's cave, reflected headlights
    slid the wall. . . . The clink of fetters: do you even
        hear it as you strain to move your neck & arms?

Connie last week at the pub sipped wine, lab coat draping
    our booth as she laughed, fresh from her seminar,
        her "Empathy Studies Symposium." They hand you

a Walkman & you're warned to never take it off, no matter
    what the voices from the tape command or caterwaul
        at you in their collective glossolalia,

ear-piercing, schizoid, but sometimes fading
    to a whisper, sometimes wholly quiet before
        feedbacking up in chimerical thunder. Imagine

the unending ebb & flow: rumor, murmur, fuck you
    & the teller hissing something terrible, which only you
        can hear & the rays from the bus driver's eyes have been

designed to mold your upper body into metal
    & thus more easily facilitate the implants
        & the toxins which will line your stomach walls.

Also, you've been issued written orders:
    buy milk & shampoo, open a checking account,
        Red Line or Blue Line to reach the Skokie Swift?

They must hold the mayo on the double cheese,
    for that's how you like it though the voices
        tell you otherwise, inform you that the dentist's drill

proceeding through your forebrain will commence
    the overture, & yellow locusts crawl your face
        presiding above the ritual murders, which must include

a second plane crash as you eat your fries against
    apartment bricks, here by the dumpster where
        you've gone because you can be alone, nearly peaceful

as the sun begins to wane. & when this couple
    strolling near the streetlight comes upon you here,
        it is crucial that you raise your head

& meet their eyes, parted lips so they will see
    your teeth. A courtesy, a warning,
        a prelude to the others which may follow.

Zola the Hobbyist: 1895

Forty grains of chloral hydrate and the subject now
may be arranged. Who has a devil in her ear

which she wishes extracted. Given to tics and grimaces,
so noted by her curate, who was of course unable

to relieve her. (The preparation of the carbon plate—
tedious work, but soothing.) Has ascended

to the ceiling at twelve each night to join
her mother, who has been dead some years.

Consternation on the husband's part, the farrier
Henri Dietz. Seven offspring, three however

stillborn. Has troubled many wardmates
in the evenings with her cries, for as she converses

with her devil others cannot sleep.
(The carbon print is not only permanent,

but renders a rich tonal scale.) Has been made
by her devil to swallow pins and buttons

and this in turn has further amplified
her cries, restraints now being required

continually, loosened only at such times
as her cries abate. (A pity about the eyes—

one would have preferred them open.) Possesses,
as you say, the expected features, lips

exceedingly thick, eye sockets set close,
to indicate a diagnosis of congestive madness.

(When dry the tissue is exposed
in contact with the negative, and then

immersed in water, together with a blank sheet of paper.)
I am pleased, my dear doctor, to hear your words

of admiration for my fiction—pleased
as a fellow scientist, for it is in such a role

that the novelist of today must regard himself.
But I must confess she has not been

our sittings' most intriguing subject—if only
the sedative had not been required!

Had I the chance to capture the eyes!
She lacks, alas, a certain mystery, a fascination.

Do I daresay her devil seems not to dwell
within the details? And would you usher, please,

the next subject in? Every man must have a hobby,
and I confess a wondrous love of mine.

And the Unclean Spirits Went Out of the Man, and Entered into Swine

(Mark 5:13)

Terrible to dwell within the body of a man
who squats in his own shit among the tombs.
Terrible his raiment, hair matted wild. Terrible the man
who wails his sorrow, scuttling in the grime
& litter of necropolis bone. O better instead to scurry
on these cloven feet, our tusks ashimmer,
better even this trance, this slither toward the sea,
the cliff where we hurl ourselves upon the breakers,
For we had tired of the ways of men & sought again
the Temple of the Four-Legged Thing, nave of sow-teat,
altar of snout & tusk, sacrament of bristle-hair, of penis bone
& musk gland. Here was our repose. But this God we bargained with,
as Gods will do, had tricked us all. & to the precipice we came.
We the exiled, We the betrayed. We whose name is Legion.

Testings, 1956

(Octet)

The booth is soundproof; the brows of the contestant knit.

◆

Before the slumber party, the girls catch thirty fireflies.

◆

Brightness first, then the poppyheaded cloud; the draftees shield their eyes.

◆

"*Dr. Faustus.*" To which the MC nods. "Exactly right."

◆

They wanted them blinking, to lantern all night the bedroom ceiling.

◆

Dr. Teller by the crater, Geiger counter hissing—water sluicing from a hose.

◆

Control booth where our sponsor paces. Hiss & murmur, murmur & hiss.

◆

Mason jars opened in the candystriped room, the thirty lights unleashing.

(Sextet)

Alchemy of sand grains fused to fist-sized stones of glass.

◆

Van Doren's been handed answers in advance. "Is it the Donner Party?"

◆

Only one to flicker toward the ceiling, its blinking unsteady.

◆

To calculate the wizening of downwind monkeys rattling cages; hair loss of the rats.

◆

"The Donner Party is exactly right!" (Cue Applause.)

◆

Morning, waking, un-Luciferian. Bedcovers spotted with dusty wings.

Pavlov's Century

"... an animal that once could run,
staring at its own tracks..."

OSIP MANDELSTAM

By many wonders was it characterized: windows graven in the mastiff's stomach,
        tawny flesh pulled back like tent flaps
To verify salivation on cue. Bells ring and the inner life commences,
        breaking down essential nutrients

before they have even passed the lips. The soul on its trail toward execution:
        good dog, companionable
& panting, aspiring to the conditioning of music. & the process may be watched,
        recorded & watched again, soul

& self in dialogue & chewing now in unison, smacking lips, so hungry
        that the plastic bowl
races back & forth across linoleum & is followed. My father learned
        to flinch from the belt buckle,

pain and its seminars, flowering from the back of the legs, then radiating
        outward, sorrowful wheel.
Here the spoke of the First Depression, proper noun, the farm foreclosed,
        here the spoke of alcohol,

gin bottle twitching down to zero & the second depression, the third & here
        the paddles against the temples,
conducting voltage, the ward room with his comb upon the nightstand.
        Soul Pavlovian, how you tremble,

for verily the stomach is the window to the soul, for the eyes are dead
        or wildly dart about

& never dead enough. Hunger & tic, & the orderly watching, bored
        but taking copious notes.

Plastic wristband, piss-smell & your gown. Here the tray is set before you, meat
        & carrots, applesauce & peas, styrofoam
chalice with its straw. Chew and swallow—it is permitted. A bell will sound
        to signal that your eating's done.

Stalin's Library Card

"A recent piece in *Pravda* gives the library books checked out by Stalin between April and December, 1926. Much has been made of their oddity . . ."

ROBERT CONQUEST

i.
The Essence of Hypnosis

(Paris: LeGrande, 1902)

The woman has agreed to swallow pins,
and here, white-robed,
                        stands great Dr. Charcot,

pointing to the needles in her palm. The photo
makes them gleam. The stovepipe-hatted amphitheatre strains,

heads abob for better looks. She's about
to lap them like sugar, but the Doctor's minion

stays her hand; down her dress they glitter and rain.
And now from the murmuring crowd he procures a hat,

placing it upon her lap.
                        Your child is crying.
Can you soothe him? Tenderly the hat's caressed.

To and fro she rocks it as she sings—a case
of "simple congestive hysteria." *He is dying,*

woman, your child is dying! The tears cascade,
her shoulders twitch and tremble. *Diagnosis confirmed.*

ii.

Syphilis: Its Detection, History, and Treatment—Illustrated

(Munich: Insel Verlag, 1922)

"The shoulders twitch and tremble at the tertiary stage,
signalling generally the advent of paresis."

Comrade Stalin tamps his pipe and struts
the carpet to the phone, having marked another passage

with red pen. *Do not put him through, I said.*
I am trying to relax. The receiver's slammed down:

collectivization can wait.
                                        He re-cracks the spine,
relights the meerschaum to Nietzsche gone mad,

to Schumann demented, to sepias of six noseless
Neapolitans, an aged whore whose arms are candle wax,

spirochetes that marinate the blood, x-es
and arrows to mark their swim. His pulse

crescendos and his forehead glistens,
x and asterisks—
                            all night the margins redden.

iii.
The Right to Kill

(Moscow: Knigoizdatel'svto Slovo, third ed., 1913)

X and asterisk: shorthand all night flowing
out the stenographer's hand. Agent Shivarov:

Why do you think we've arrested you? He cups
his face in his hands while Mandelstam fidgets, blowing

on his tea to cool it.
                    Could it be your poems?
(The bulb's faint hum, the stenographer's cough.)

On the desk a bulging file, from which Shivarov
removes a smudged carbon, sliding it toward Mandelstam

along the tabletop. *A recitation, please?*
The hand begins to quiver as the carbon blues

his palm—
                    "the Kremlin mountaineer . . . the thick worms
of his fingers . . . executions on his tongue like berries."

*Do you recognize yourself as guilty of composing tracts
of counter-revolutionary nature?* And the blue hand shakes.

iv.
Is Resurrection of the Dead Possible?

(London: Theosophy International, 1921)

Against the table the cadaver thrashes: its blue arms quiver—
a little. More voltage to the genitals
and a kind of erection is achieved, which Dr. Lysenko
duly notes, yet Lazarus does not stir,

exactly.
        One week to Comrade Stalin's visit,
and the demonstrations must impress:

too much voltage and the corpses combust,
too little and the limbs remain inert

as noodles. Notes scratched on his clipboard, the doctor
scowls to his shuffling assistant, who hits

the switch.
        And Lazarus sizzles—flames emit
from the electroded temples. The good doctor swears

and flails his arms, as the corpse performs
its own suttee. The corpse has the final word.

Ritual Murder Among the Jews

(St. Petersburg: Parizh, 1910)

Do not wait until we force you: we will have the final say.
Begin your confession.
                    Precise as a slide rule

and always natural as the smell of dill—
interrogation, too, is art. Babel sways

upon his stool, his neck goes limp. The aesthetics
of confession must be formalist:

The Trotskyite Babel will weep and stutter but list
in the end his cohort spies.
                        Yet first he must wake.

Cold water to the face, a truncheon to the legs
and his writer's block is over. The singing

commences with the truncheon's sting,
the singing and the singing and the singing—

its own dark Kaddish, its own crematorium smoke.
The verdict is final, the case is closed.

vi.
Practical Versification

(Moscow: Khudozhestvennoy Literaturiy, 1908)

Should the couplets be open or should they be closed?
The day requires signatures, decrees.

He longs for verse, but must speak in prose.
All the endless signatures.
       A photo shoot: he poses

with pen in hand, the *Pravda* newsman on his knees.
Should the couplets be open or should they be closed?

Signatures of every sort, the pace never slows.
The State revised, rewritten endlessly.

He hungers for verse but lives by prose,
redrafted, retouched. The coffins set in rows

like Red Square parades, marching to infinity.
Should the couplets be open
       or should they be closed?

Late in the Kremlin, his desk lamp glows.
So much to excise, he's up until three.

(O to live by verse instead of prose. . . .)
The drafts soar upward. On his desk the pile grows

skyscraper high, Babel tower and gallows tree.
O sentence in verse, o sentence in prose.

Should the couplets be open or should they be closed?

vii.
Proposal for Revision of the First Soviet Encyclopedia

(Moscow: Sovietsky Pisatel, 1926)

The people can be made to swallow anything.
For example Comrade Yezhov,
$$\text{Special Marshal}$$

of the Secret Police, has been shot. He will
now require closure, require editing.

His service to the party, his Trotskyite past,
all must now be excised, even his birth

converted to white space.
$$\text{But first}$$
his face must pentimento down to nothingness.

No longer can he pose with Comrade Stalin
admiring the Moscow-Volga Canal. Now he is water.

No longer at His right in parades at Red Square.
Now he is air, is brickwork on the viewing stand.

And now the past itself is air, is water, and finally fire,
whitening to ash.
In his fat fingers its pages flare.

Tribulation Eclogue

On a leaf they couple, faint pulsations pillowed by my palm—
like signals from deep space. The male lumbers up her carapace,
needle feelers jackknifing as he throbs, legs rowing air,

exquisite in their way, colliding firmaments, lacquer-black
& clotted with stars. In their world this is accompanied
by growl & cry, undetectable by me, piling up branches

from the storm, downed tree on a streetlight, linemen working chainsaws
up the block to bring back power. I will suffocate them in a jar
& hand them over to Cook County like extradited terrorists.

Asian Spotted Longhorn Beetles, & the neighborhood's
in quarantine. In five years every tree in Illinois
is theirs—no known predators, effective insecticides,

or way to lure them into traps. Stowawayed from Shanghai
& Maceió in packing crates, they'll eat their tunnels into heartwood,
cancering down the largest trunks. *O great Nineveh,*

the fire shall devour Thee, the cankerworm shall eat Thee up,
shall spoileth & fleeth away. The myrrh-anointed beard
of Ashurbanipal shall glitter into flame & beneath the chariot wheels

his perfumed raiment shall be trodden. The forking paths of empire
all slither down into the same Ozymandiac trash compactor
hydraulicing impounded cars into impossible steel fists,

teetering three stories high, layers like Troy or Jericho.
The neighbor's Lab howls at the linemen endlessly.
Feelers akimbo, they claw the mason jar walls. Yet they are properly

addressed as Sire, as Marduk & many-armed Shiva,
& Kali of the necklace forged of gleaming skulls
His Consort. I have seen the rainforest only once

& count myself among the last. Past Cairns & the tourist hotels,
the road gives way to mangrove swamps. You cross the Daintree
in a ferry scabrous with rust & swatting flies the Aussie

newsman asks Yusef if Simpson will get off. Fan palms
spew mist, the tendon of the ferry cable groaning as a croc's snout
cruises our wake. He yammers on about the bloody glove,

slap of the sawtoothed tail submerging. Stinging tree,
Goanna slinking to a hole, Yusef on his knees with the Nikon
beneath the ferns' huge treble clefs, all of us canopied,

lime-colored light & the palms' strict shadows slicing down.
Walking stick: the long green thorax zigzags up the pantleg
of our guide, who bends to a steamy cassowary turd,

poking it with tweezers to display the insides brimming
with seeds like a rotten melon. Upon such black, endangered,
visionary shit, this jungle's frail ecology depends,

bejeweled with flies, ants in legion plundering seeds.
& now the trees give way to shoreline. Low tide
& we pick our way across the moonscape of a dead coral reef,

pocked & gray & featureless for miles, pacing a corpse
as large as a city, barnacle-fettered, clumped with algae,
the Aussies' camera shutters clicking fast as castanets

until the tide returns, the reef ashimmer. O body of Marsyas,
singing still & flayed, skinned by pesticide, groundwater run-off
from Port Douglas canefields, a hundred miles south.

& the tide is bearing down on us. Stumbling we slither
the endless torso, aiming for the trees. On this very bay
Cook's *Endeavour* ran aground. & here they lay in fever

seven months. *Stranded upon this barbarous coast we stayed,*
imperilled always by rapacious savages. I thus have named this place
Cape Tribulation, for here our sorrows began in earnest.

for Yusef Komunyakaa

The Art of Poetry

(for Roger Mitchell)

In the beginning, desolation everywhere.
Hulking, glaciered, dishwater gray, the rocks
loom up from a spit of beach.
Here the men will winter & await the rescue ship,
relieved to stand at last
on solid ground. Eleven months
they've drifted on the floes, *Endurance*
squeezed to sticks of timber as the pack ice
tightened: "Elephant Island."
Shackleton may save them or he may
be dead. & everyone is sick to death
of penguin steaks. On "Mount Snowden"
they've set their flag, & in the hour
of August twilight that is day, they scan
the berged horizon for a sail
or swath of smoke, they gobble
imagined feasts. Today, a Yorkshire pudding,
conjured Homerically; gravy bubbling
on the dumplings & potatoes,
aubergines in curry & a starrygazy pie,
apple tarts, the Devonshire cream aswirl.
Great buckets of claret & frothy Guinness
wash it down. The Woodbines
& cigars are lit, brandy in the club rooms
& the smoking cars. Blackboro's
right foot may well be saved,
but the toes of the left are surely gangrenous.
So on this first warm windless day
the main tent is cleared, hoosh pot
filled with ice to boil & crates in a line
make a kind of gurney. Penguin skins

sizzle white on the stove, & all the blubber lamps
glow. Macklin & McIlroy strip
to undershirts & Blackboro breathes
huge draughts of chloroform. His toes
are black, the flesh almost mummified.
Now the incision, snaking & laborious
along the foot. McIlroy peels back
the skin. He tests the forceps & the toes
spin down into a bucket,
clanging one by one. Blackboro,
waking groggy, wants a smoke. Will someone
please read to him awhile? & from
the salvaged three-book library
they choose *Britannica, N–O*. Numerology
gives way to Numismatics, McIlroy
bending in the lamp glow
to point out burnished coins
in rows, Xerxes & a Ptolemy
with laurel crown. The Nutmeg
is tropical, hard & aromatic
is its seed. Blackboro drifting,
his hands unmittened & from Nutrition
come the Nymphs: Dryads who haunt
the forests & groves, Leimoniads the meadows
& in waters dwell the Naiads, Potamids
& Hydriads. But Nyx, thrice-great Nyx,
world-making Nyx, of whose breath
the earth & firmament were formed, whose realm
is All Things Of The Night, born of Chaos
& Mother of Aether, is a goddess
most fearsome, even by Zeus revered.

II

Poison, 1959

Sixteen wasps against a fallen apple, hissing green,

◆

bejeweled & dappled. A child can bend

◆

to their seething, astonished as they drain

◆

the sweet fermenting juices. But insecticide

◆

can change them utterly & the child can briefly

◆

consider God, now incarnate as Himself,

◆

God-of-Pillar-of-Smoke-from-Heaven-DDT

◆

(in those days the poison of choice) & He sprays. Strafed

◆

they mutate, strafed they still. & what child

◆

does not covet many eyes, to weave & hover,

◆

weave & sting, to expel like breath miraculous paper & build

◆

for himself a palace wondrous strange & infinitely chambered?

◆

Of many eyes the world is made. Infinite are its wishes

◆

& its sibilant wings. Therefore they each must perish.

The Ravenswood

Yellow tint of nicotine
        around the scarlet lacquer
                of her nails. The el
lurches forward.
      From the plate glass I can see
             the engine sway the curve
& bend the shadows of the cars
        against the Rosehill cenotaphs
              & mausoleums below;
pillars, broken capitals.
       She's dozing with a crushproof in her fist.
             Henna & crazy rouge,
fur pillbox to match her shawl:
       five black-snouted,
          amber-eyed-mink,
to which, when she wakes,
      she seems to be talking,
         hospital wristband glinting
as she lifts her arm,
     gangsta seeping from
        the headphones of the kid beside me.
Grim florid music of rebus
      to which I too
        am captive:
Mother you are dead ten years
      & the dining car
        will close in fifteen minutes
in October 1960,
    halfway to Seattle for a funeral
        & the Northwest Limited
grates upon its grindstone

westward for days.

                    I've been asleep

against her shoulder

        cheek beside the glistening fur

                      she's unhooked

& pillowed for me, eyes to the golden

                unblinking eyes,

                        stitched mouths downy

& talcum & Shalimar.

        I crane my neck,

                the engine in twilight

leaning the curve.

        We've been waiting for the tunnel,

                      one point seven

miles long,

     both fighting sleep,

                the fur & her smell so close

they are breathing me,

            erection

            (but I'm too young

to call it that)

        warm inside my dungarees.

                      Against her arm,

against her dozing arm,

            the Salem she lit

                pulsing down.

For nine days,

        lifetime upon lifetime,

                The Rebel Angels

plummeted,

      tenfold confusion in their fall,

                downward rush, clamorous

whistle of skin rent endlessly.

        Headlong, says Milton,

                headlong themselves

they threw.
   Against your arm,
       against your dozing arm.
The tunnel yawning
     receives us whole.
         Sting of menthol,
Shalimar, birthmark,
     sweet abrasions
        bristling my neck,
bringing me your profile back.
      Then vortex, spasm,
          sudden dark
within the car.
    The glow, the flicker.
      Ash.

Word Horde against the Gnostics

Into error so often led. Founded in error, as it is written
    in *The Gospel of Truth*,
The Paraphrase of Shem, The Second Apocalypse of James. Father
    Creator lost, shrouded in mist,

& these gods who are Gods of Error, who have founded (so it
    is written)
this day, which is the car lot phone across Norwood, stuttering
    loud enough to rattle

my windowpanes, the summer asphalt asmolder. Which is the blind man
    being led by his son along
the fenders & grease pencil tractates pocking windshields: WOW
    & BEAUT & FACTORY AIR.

And Anguish grew solid like a fog, so that no one was able to see,
    which is lawnsprinkler's cat hiss,
gelignite, ebola, battering ram, the influenza outbreak of 1918,
    & a hand working up

the antenna, over black lacquer grilles of 'stangs & Z-28s.
    Something for his boy
to make him one with & one with. Flap of pennants which he hears
    & the boy ignores,

& my own hands fumbling the keyboard at my window, spendthrift
    also in their error, which is,
which is, which is. *For this reason Error grew powerful,*
    not having known the truth.

It fashioned its own matter, and Error did grow enraged at Him
   and He was nailed
to a tree . . . Which is attack dog, labyrinth, applause, stuck pig
   dangling from its feet on the trolley

of the Armour & Co. aerial railway, Dreiser by the "red-headed
   giant" butcher dodging blood,
the senile ex-President all smiles beside the actors in three-
   cornered hats, the cameras agog.

Sorrowful wheel. Word horde you jotted still living on
   the inside cover of Hart Crane,
for me to unearth this morning two years beyond. But say we can
   love this error, the one with

& the one with, book aslant on the desktop & flecked with
   your cursive, the imitation
leather seat, hand on the shiftknob & the powertop creaking down,
   salesman adjusting & glint

of the blind man's shades. Soon the check written out by the boy
   who will guide his father's hand to sign.
& soon the laser scanning the true-leather voice of Joey Ramone—
   Didn't you love that?—until

the speakers throb, how *Needles a-a-and pins hurt* . . . spendthrift
   in their error. Then segue
to the silken lamentations of Sam Cooke, begging *to just touch* . . .
   the hem of His garment . . . O say

we love this spendthrift error, this want, this lack, this key now
   jazzing the ignition,
top down & the deal made. *Tarnish, apples, tabloid, x-ray.*
   My hands along the keyboard & swirl

of hairpin turns. *Hyacinth, shoulders, tango, leotard, Grand Hotel,*
    perfected, invisible ink.
Shades off & the wind against the eyes, useless & holy & beautiful
    error lets out the clutch, three chords

slithering their sacred din. O Founded Powers hear me:
    look You now upon these wonders.

After Propertius

(IV.7, Sunt aliquid Manes: letum non omnia finit)

Ghosts do exist. Ash & bone-stubble, we left her pyre
    smoldering, libations
where the flames contusioned skyward. We piled the battered
    red thesaurus, & then

her jewelry, her father's bee books. Toga-shroud & camphor wood, Cynthia
    now was shade, slithering colorless from smoke.
& on my bed I'd mourn each night before I slept—brass four-poster
    where we groaned delirious fucks.

& it was here her phantom swayed above me in my dream. *Wake up*
    Propertius, wake up, you shit
& look upon your Cynthia. Asleep already? The hair, her eyes—
    exactly as they'd been upon her shroud:

three years ago to this day. Patchouli-smell, lapis ring afloat
    before me, fire-gnawed & battered.
Wrist-bones clicking, humeri a-rattle. *How goes the poetry, loverboy? Did I give*
    good subject matter?

Don't think I haven't heard your three-year keening. & now it's given you—
    I've given you—another little book.
Yes, I've read it; not much else to do in Hades' endless cellblocks
    but unscroll papyri; nobody here shoots up,

wine's beside the point, & fucking means nada to a crew with coins
    so heavy on their ectoplasmic tongues.
Desire is for amateurs, & shame. Imagine it, Propertius, that I
    of all people am beyond

such things: though you, I see, have hardly changed at all: Mr. Legendary
  Piss & Moan. Give me a break.
How loose the mourning-toga hung upon her bones, & her turban,
  shot-through with golden thread,

floated glistening & unscorched, as did her eyes, gunmetal blue—
  flaring with the gaze that always shone
on me & with the same prodigious rage. *It's time, Propertius,*
  for a little travelogue.

Outside the Trailways station you'll find Cerberus asleep; he's mangy,
  a toothless shepherd-boxer mix,
jaws always working while he dreams of prey—waterfront rats
  most likely. & Styx?

Think Boston & the Combat Zone, but before it a shit-oozing smell
  from the flooded street, where Charon
(aka "Dr. Nods," aka "Tugboat") pulls the fillings from your mouth
  with pliers (though there is no pain),

& with his gold tooth shining, his 'fro sprawling beachball-size, he leads
  you on the stepping-stones
he's made of car hoods, dumpster covers. & now you'll hover on
  The Other Side, floating along

the mentholed air, past "25 Cent Movies," GIRLS! GIRLS! GIRLS!
  ADONIS THEATRE preening its neon.
& suddenly you know Hart Crane is here, Chet Baker, Clytemnestra, Emily
  & Medea. & then

before you, dear Propertius, looms your SRO, its TRANSIENTS
  WELCOME pulsing & its lobby
sporting zoot suits, eye patches, hot-panted legs uncrossing, gang
  tattoos; arm-pit stink & every eye

fixed maybe on the Zenith with its sound turned down, maybe on
   the umbrella stand, bristling with canes,
prosthetic legs. The desk clerk's been expecting you. One milky eye,
   & his pinky-ringed hand holds out your key.

"With tears in death we ratify life's loves," he says. (At least
   the sense of irony remains
intact.) The elevator's broken; you can use the stairs. Begin
   your climb, Propertius. Begin.

"Asend the Stare: On Top Floor Please Ring Bell"

(Cavafy Museum, Alexandria)

As if Christo wrapped the courtyard stairs with dripping sheets

◆

& traffic noise, from where your guide has circled, lost. & off the tourist

◆

map, as you suppose it always shall be. Pinstripe-narrow street

◆

("bordello for the Flesh & church for Sin—& the hospital

◆

where you go to die"), chair upturned on the cafe table, polis of little intrigues, Ptolemaic

◆

gossip, & the boys (so beautiful) on the cusp of ruin. & his pen, to balance

◆

the Yes & the No—Adonis losing at 3-card monte, but chiseled immortal in mimeograph

◆

& stapled in a pamphlet to the poet's name. & the moist sheets ripple, valanced

◆

with handkerchiefs & socks, stained faintly, salted with the pathos

◆

of human fluids. & the cotton t-shirts, roiling in a line, graven still with the shapes

◆

of pectorals, tremor of nipple & the clothespinned sleeves. O pentimentoed

◆

tan lines & the torsos resplendent, white in attic marble & white on the beaches

◆

of el-Montazah where the rough & temporal Gods still throng.

◆

Above dwells Eros, whose province is Longing. Part these curtains and ascend.

Firstborn of Egypt

As breath the angel comes, as droplets of mist
◆
coalescing to evoke a form, fish schools
◆
mimicking the shark. Breath beneath the door,
◆
the angel swirls, in sorrow avenging. & some of us
◆
have borne His Mark. & many o many shall wail.
◆
& at what moment, o Dark One, are we Marked by Thee? Over
◆
which unclouding mirror, which thrumming fluoroscope
◆
pulsing our withered hands, pewter and kinetic, fossil fish?
◆
Over which page 20 of *The Bridge,* scored with spidery cursive
◆
all about the margins, hers? Flame-rinsed needles, ice.
◆
She had pierced my ear & now she lay against
◆
my chest, sleeping & alive. & none shall be saved.
◆
The sting, gold stud I wore for years. The Mark, o Angel
◆
of those Ye take.
                    & the Mark of those who wail.

Days of 1994

They wanted rehab—at least a month from her,
not just the writhing days it took for detox.

& anyway by this time it was all a kind of joke:
on the third day she would rise again, transfigured,

to sign herself out. & with the plastic bracelet
still dot-matrixing her name, band inching white

from her black leather jacket, she spat out
curses at the liquor store clerk, who'd told her that

she looked as though she'd already had enough.
Corners where she'd score after teaching

her expensive undergrads to bring
more spondees to their closures. Kitchen floor she'd strafe

& pockmark with her cane. & the bed in the attic room
where I & various others held her nightlong

through the shakes. Heavy the burden
she took upon herself those final days. But calm

& plaintive was her final singing. Track-marked arms
& jet-black sleeves within the coffin silk,

her lips made florid in the mortuary light, kissed
& wept upon by many, who would write their brittle poems

to stylize their grief for her, as if her death
could belong to them as well. O days of 1994,

bring back to me her quickened human form,
even in her fevers & the tremor & exactness

of her curses. Bring back to me the dampened cloth
I wring out in a bowl, cheekbone & clavicle,

as her eyelids flutter & her forehead at last grows cool.
Bring back this broken fever. Let the others have the rest.

For the Centenary of Hart Crane

i.

Grace Hart Crane Calls up the Shades: A Séance, 1935

"Mother, you would be surprised to know that here
we voyage nowhere & our words are dross.

Sometimes of course we speak to one another
but in a kind of stage whisper as we float

back & forth, balloons atop a swimming pool.
(My metaphors have gotten . . . buoyant.)
                                        So your request

for my 'unwritten poems' leaves me a little
cold, if you'll pardon the pun. Perhaps it's best

they remain unrecorded, although
I know you need the solace
                              of some cash.

My Cortez epic would have been a wreck. My odes
to pricks of cabin boys would make you flinch,

poison to *Criterion* & *Dial.* All their delicate
jaws would drop!
                    But here's one, Mother. It goes like this:"

ii.
Crane Writing Ad Copy: Manhattan, 1923

His ode to the Pittsburgh Water Heater praises
"dependability & long life."
                                        Over

& over he's labored a sentence, a katabasis
of bumpkin prose. Next month the *Orizaba*

sails for Havana, but today it's warranties
anviled & alchemized to dulcet song.

A fifth of hidden Cutty in his desk will ease
the boredom & the shakes,
                                        while Henry Vaughan

gets paged for lunch, *White Devil* through the coffee break.
His father's letter burns his pocket—

"Harold, do you think I'm *made* of money?" Specs
of the Heat-o-matic, drafts of his reply: "Never mock

my calling, Father: *I am made of words.*" Punch-out:
unsteady down the subway steps he floats.

iii.
Crane at Factoria del Cigaros: Havana, 1926

"When you call for the rollers of big see-gars in truth,
the room's vast as a zeppelin hangar. Hot

as sizzling butter. They hunch in rows, their mouths
stitched shut.
                    Only the ceiling fans' rat-tat-tat

& the voice of The Reader, seated on a kind of dais
galumphing through an Edgar Rice Burroughs,

hand gestures galore: *Tarzan y el Pais
Perdido.*
          Cantatas from their wrists, the stogies flow

year upon year, through every Tarzan, every Dumas:
word as betel nut, page as aromatic snorts

of nicotine. In time their hands themselves turn ash.
Ashes to ashes, prose to prose. The art

of poetry here breaks down. O tongueless bell, a-toll for no one.
Basta! Basta!
              Forgive me the done, the left undone."

iv.
At the Blessing of the Animals: Taxco, Xmas, 1932

The white cat can't abide her earrings nor
her blotchy slather of pink dye. Turkeys

peck their tinsel chain mail & the taxi burros
sport sombreros, bullwhipping tails at flies.

Craveted monkeys scold at green *pericos*
& Hart's lost Peggy in the sweat-drenched throng.

Mescal-addled, seeing double, he perches
on a wall to spy her,
              like a figure on the railing

of a ghost ship, figurehead weathering some private tempest,
reefward spiralling. Mariachi blare,

the tower bells' spindrift oversong. As the blessed
exeunt the ark,

    he catches a glimpse of her.

Then she's lost again to the braying tidal clamor
hissing out the church doors to the bestial square.

v.
A Grave in Garrettsville: 1989

Stone Age, Bronze Age, Age of Iron,
Age of Voyage, Age of Cable

      arcing rivers.

But Age of Silver thine. Age of Gold, which burns,
of course, the tongue. Age of Night-Shake Terror.

Age of L. and I, who'd driven hours, arguing.
& Age of Stone *redux*, where *Lost At Sea*

was sudden rockdrilled granite, *HAROLD HART CRANE*.
& L. half-smashed,

    with garlands, on one knee,

five years to live. No sexton led us. Compassless,
we'd staggered 'til your plot loomed up,

landlocked among oaks, the drought-shriven grass.
Fabled shadow, the sea still keeps you. Drowned book,

the sod & sea & twilight keep a counsel of their own.
To salt we commended thee

     & all night drove toward home.

Dirge with Proofs

Kerosene & cowshit & a rented truck, heavy-laden

◆

& we have "a low-order explosive device."

◆

Remote engaged. Radio waves, surfing to detonation.

◆

Pockmarked sky, the color of a bruise,

◆

then recoil, the building's trepanned north side.

◆

Working your proofs, second set: I misread *crucial* for *cruel*,

◆

this for your description of *the world,*

◆

burning crucial, burning ruthless. The feral

◆

blood-compounded cry, the child in the rescue worker's

◆

lemon & black asbestos gloves, the wail

◆

precise, articulate as theorems. They stagger

◆

cameraward. The screen goes dark as braille.

◆

Book to be read in the dark. Book-of-the-Abyss.

◆

Crucial world, only world. Pomegranate seed. The famished goddess.

Spirit Cabinet

House-of-Justice-One-Way-Glass: you can't see in, not to the upper floors,
    where cell rows mean to prove
that here blind justice is half cured. For the sake of morale the inmates
    are permitted to see out—

the liquor store & coffee bar, haircut salon which goes by the name
    of Mondo. & thus the women
on the sidewalk lift their baby daughters up, allowing the men
    to view them from their cells.

I have seen them on my morning run—hard-faced women with beer logo t-shirts,
    stick-thin from the crystal
& the cigarettes, who chalk on the concrete missives to husbands, to boyfriends
    caught raising weed, or tending

chicken shack meth labs. So LOVE YOU DADDY's framed by daf
    & hyacinth bouquets,
now in the early stages of rot. Ah, the sightings of the world beyond
    arise with suddenness & pain.

Rough winds shake our offerings, unpetalled to the whirlwind, whose ears
    are indifferent to such pleas
as we may utter. Upon the death of Mother Ann Lee the Shakers were bereft,
    crying for weeks,

lamentations unending, seeking in their tremors & mortifications to raise her up,
    uncorrupted still. The planks
of the meetinghouse floor for days did tremble, circle dance unceasing
    in its bow & jerk & whirl.

Upon the floor they fell to writhing & held forth for weeks in languages unknown,
    communing with spirits
both good & ill, & built of cherrywood & burnished maple
    the *Spirit Cabinets,*

contraptions half altar & half library carrel, in front of which believers
    would entrance themselves,
awaiting orders from beyond. To many brethren Mother Lee did show herself,
    to many others she did not.

& how, o spirits, shall I invoke you, who cannot count himself
    among the chosen?
My writhings & keenings are interior & treated by appropriate
    prescription drugs,

to whom my conversion is incomplete, for some days I devote myself
    solely to my dead
& in my error I do seek them & do wail. From the wire mesh
    I glimpse the chalk marks,

aflicker on a kind of slate. Here is the glyph of patchouli-smell,
    graven on a scarf
or silken dress. & here the character for a chin nicked while shaving,
    stubble edging a dime-sized birthmark,

too tender to give over to the razor. Hieroglyphic of a bedside table, lipstick
    on a gin glass by her smokes.
My slate, my singing slate, my Spirit Cabinet, fragrant of rosin
    & sawdust & glue,

clairvoyant to channel the many-tongued chorus. My dead, my alphabet,
    my Mondo Morte,
my burning chalk which breaks the night, hear me & forgive me
    in my thrall & error.

III

Crayola: A Sequence

i.

Sangre I: Bleeding Out

Roommate's appendix on the bedstand: it helixes

◆   **hemorrhage after tonsillectomy**

8/58

& quivers, caterpillars butter-colored liquid,

◆

jar-glint as Nurse Rachel works the blinds

◆

& my eyes dazzle, sunstruck. Type O Negative

black & white

◆   **Chuck Connors**

slithers rubied toward my bandaged hand,

◆

purple bruises lacing out beneath the gauze.

◆

as *The Rifleman*

I'd almost bled out. Now just chills & fevers   **then blackout**

◆

but last night a scarlet rivulet foamed my chin,

the World of Spirits

is not heaven nor hell

◆

white dresses clamoring the bed, code blue

but a state intermediate

◆   **betwixt the two**

twilit half-awake, glimpses of their laving hands.

◆

Up a chute my soul streaks ashen, cindered

◆

& from which after a suitable time

& dispersing into God-Eye White Light Bardo   **we shall be either**

◆

Little Star atwinkle, *David David David,*

                                                   raised upward onto heaven

       ◆   **or casteth down unto hell**

head ragdolling eyeless in some orderly's arms

       ◆

& then I jolt awake, corporeal again, stream   **Chrysler Imperial Winston**

                                  Tastes Good

       ◆

of Type O sluicing our chests, laud, red laud, incarnadined.

                                 Rifleman's gun blazing

                                      through it all

ii.
With Divers Illustrations

The staff becomes a serpent, the serpent again a staff.

◆

Here the Tree of Knowledge, stunted pear in the yard

Children's Bible, c.
1940s

◆

of my grandmother watching Ike. Goliath's head uplifted drips.

illus.
Feodor Rojankovsky

The kitchen table, scored for years by knives, crosshatched

◆

like oracle bones. Requisite sepias—the grim-faced dead.

◆

But from the fiery furnace three were saved

Klondike is also known
under a variety of local names

◆

Dead aunt on the porch swing shuffling cards.

Fascination Demon Patience
Chinaman

Blackberries scaling the fence empurpled & our mouths are stained.

◆

Shadrach, Meshach, Abednego: from the furnace they came

& Nebuchadnezzar
was full of fury

◆

to high office in Babylon. & the windows quivered

◆

Boxcar doors ajar
shuffling light

each time the freights bore down—August dust,

◆

ozone smell & diesel, frogs overrunning Karnak,

◆

Nile foaming blood, & on the garden paths,

◆

blue-robed, blazing golden light, God is seen to walk.   **grandiose Tolstoyan beard**

◆

The odor which portends rain. The knitting needles click,

◆

lapis ring, the gnarled hand. *The serpent tempted and I ate.*

Cherubim & a flaming sword

iii.
Recollection Including a Textbook Quotation

Turbaned, bathrobed, she shuffled in, "agitated"

◆

(my mother's term) no more. The operation

prone to temper tantrums
& willfulness before

◆

had seen to that, bruise on her forehead

◆

tiny as a shaving nick. The visiting room—ceiling fan

◆

the animal seemed to become
almost cheery after

hissing shadows on the mah-jongg tiles. They'd changed

◆

her mind for good. Cousin Beatrice. Test pattern on the Motorola

◆

when stirred back & forth

at which a bald man peered. Blue eyes, lipstick, "Ginny, David,

◆

they told me you might . . ." I gazed at my RC Cola

the leukotomy would destroy
the nerve fibers

◆

ice cubes shrinking, mirroring the fan above. "How good,

◆

How good, they said you might." Our Lady of Faribault

◆

of the Seven Thousand Beds, hers being one. The red

in which tiles
are drawn and discarded

◆

lips thanked us for the chocolates. "Mah-jongg—have you ever played?"

◆

The surgical tools. . . often included. . . an icepick.

until one player secures

◆

the winning hand

(I hadn't, but they taught me.) Fat raindrops. Her doctor's name was Merrick.

◆

"An office procedure, really." More rain & our tiles clicked.   1931–?

◆

"Such a gentleman," she said. Through the whole operation she'd been awake.

iv.
Marvel, Eschatology, Transistor

Comics in the fallout shelter with its folding lawnchairs—

wind machine howling

soundtrack splintering glass

canned goods, batteries, bottled water, sacks of rice. My place

◆

to sneak to read Green Lantern & The Flash in peace.

the householder

is blown out of our vision

(The door bolts from the inside, to stave off Khruschev's soldiers.)

◆

Even the stout-hearted

DC & Marvel, to my mother = *trash*.   ***Emerald Gladiator***

finally succumbs

◆

Flash, what's wrong
with me . . . ?

But I'd rather be here superheroing. The *Classics*

◆

Illustrateds which she sanctions are a snooze. O texts

Brace yourself, Green Lantern
you have been *stricken*

◆

(which wire me later with a taste for porn), O Flash

◆

Give me your *power ring*
with it I will try

by flashlight in the locked cell, horizontal streaks

◆

to prevent the *plague*
from carrying you off

extruding winglike from his back to signal speed.

◆

The Tokens from the Bakelite transistor as I read

charts #1 10/62

week of Cuban Missile Crisis

◆

falsetto that Tonight The Lion Sleeps:

◆

weem-a-wei, a-weem-a-wei, a-weem-a-wei & so forth

◆

Weialala leia

Wallala leialala

like the Thames Daughters' doo-wop in the Fire Sermon.

◆

The Lion Sleeps. Save us from the Reds, Green Lantern,

◆

To Carthage then I came

from hair loss & Ground Zero, Flash. O Lion, my sepulcher is locked.

burning burning

Tiresias & Crayola

The Blind Man has a braille watch. It clamshells open

◆

Figure of Mankind in the Dark Cave

when he strokes it, report like a popping blister,   **here they have been since childhood**

◆

canary-throat sucking a dropper. Afternoons, my mother

◆

reads to him, 50 cents an hour. The North Koreans

legs and necks chained so they

◆   **cannot move distant fire blazing**

torched his eyes to lacquer. (Mother allows he's a little nuts.)

◆

Sitterless days, I tag along, Crayola Deluxe Box,

64 *Tru-To-Life Hues*

◆   ***Mask of Zorro* coloring book**

no gum (he can *hear* me chew), *Argosy Colliers Look.*

◆

The living room is shadow, his face seared meat.

Sputnik What It Means

◆   **To Science**

Fingers cane, sniffs as she flips the pages. "Burnt Sienna," "Flesh,"

◆

& "Salmon": I try to stay inside the lines. Then mumble & snort

◆

crescendoing, duetting with her voice. *Gin, I smell it smell it.*

◆

Did you just you're wet come in from fucking him? I can taste

will he not fancy that

◆   **the shadows which he formerly saw**

you from across the room. Then *Please Wayne Please Wayne*

◆

think about the boy. Rocking now, rocking, scarred hands to his skull.

are truer than the objects

◆

which now are shown to him

Then what? Coats on, leaving? Or does she rise to stroke his temples,

Sammy Davis Jr. A Day With

◆

Mr. Entertainment

start again on *Look?* "Forest," "Puce": I try to keep inside the lines.

1927?–?

vi.
Rime of the New Types of Weaponry

Specifically the metal swing seat, caroming to its target:

        ◆

Kevin Kubala's dimwit mug. His gullet commences

        ◆

its air raid drill. I aim again. He twitches

        ◆

over the grass, sirening louder. I parrot

        ◆

his yowling, salting his wounds. In Xanadu

        ◆

did Kevin Kubala with bloody cranial dome

        ◆

zig zag limping, bawling his path toward home.

        ◆

Stitches required: seven. The whole Kubala crew—

        ◆

Mr., Mrs., Kevin—marches from Porlock

        ◆

to our doorstep, Kevin helmeted in gauze.

        ◆

Words exchanged, my mother scowling. Problem of *Impulse*

        ◆

new types of weapons
& armor came into use

at the end of the
LH IIIB period

the umpire takes his place
word is given

& immediately there follow
five rapid clashes of the sabers

the whole interest is centered
on watching the wounds

they come always in one
of two places

Control (Mr. K's had teacher college). When the door's locked   **on the top of the head**
or the left side of the face

◆

she quick-draws the slipper, emptying its chambers,

◆

entrance wounds sizzling across my white rear. 79 Dahlia,   **the ship hath been**
suddenly becalmed

◆

Mahtomedi, Minnesota. Kevin's hairless from leukemia

◆

by fall. Doughnuts at his funeral, my navy blue blazer.

& the albatross
begins to be avenged

vii.
Bedtime Reading: Pictograph & Dog Ear

Triangle dog ear: that's what he teaches me. The book

◆

A Boy's Book of Alexander
Sir Nigel Fox

has just begun; already I'm fighting sleep. Eye-patch

◆

of Philip of Macedon. Pausanias unsheathes his knife

◆

(no, *dagger*)—until tomorrow it will plunge into his back.

◆

Monochrome green, like a dollar bill. Pictures head the chapters,

Linguists term this
decisive innovation

◆

none in color. Wets his finger: *this will mark our place*

which underlies
puns today

◆

& I place my hand on his, our hands now on the crease

the rebus principle

◆

that binds us, hinged like the bathroom door

◆

& the tub where in steam I soap his back. Wine-dark mole

genitalia floating
soapy water

◆

below his neck, shoulder's rose tattoo that glistens,

Boot Camp '42-43 (?)

◆

pulses in hothouse vapor. Pale skin, then the blinding crimson

◆

Shaving brush Noxzema
petalling toward me as I scrub in circles: **eucalyptus smell**

◆

dog ear, rebus, pictograph. Then he leaves me with the light

◆

still glowing. All night the dagger will plunge

Night terrors stop age 7

◆

through my sleep. Persepolis and Nineveh shall burn

◆

from Alexander's torches. O see the gilded palaces ignite.

Murder of Darius,
BC 331

viii.
First Death in Minnesota

Color of pine-pitch, the jackalope's eyes lord the mantelpiece. Rub them,

◆

The character of the antediluvian

is melancholy

drill your fingers through the sockets, but the stare is unperturbed—

◆

accusing, horned like Moses, stern as Uncle Emil. & sore afraid I am,

◆

E. A. Wojahn

& Son Taxidermy

eyes that tell me everything I know is wrong. Muzzle curled,

◆

& Knives Sharpened

While U Wait

fanged & wired into permanent snarl. & down the cellar

◆

planks we creak: Uncle Emil's workshop, dirt-floor

Toward the end of the papyrus

the deceased now mummified is told

◆

smell, potato peel & eye: Felaheen and Howard Carter

◆

with torches downward to the tomb. But now Let There

The Gods of the Openings adore Thee

They rejoice to see Thy Form

◆

Be Light: fluorescent tube's slow boil, table, sawdust, scalpel,

◆

Two Hundred Six jars of fat

owl, fox & chickenhawk, lynx in mid-stride & and the smell   **were boiled down to produce**

◆

writhing sick-sweet up our nostrils. With a flourish Uncle Emil

the frankincense & cedar oil & other balms

◆

unfolds his *White Bear Press*: inside, a sleeping rabbit. The table

◆

quivers as he makes the cut, easy as a zipper

◆

until the fur hangs loose, sawdust-flecked, a grocery sack

◆

a-bristle with hair. The slithering rubied insides make me sick

◆

& Uncle Emil grins. Upward I plummet, the hiss of the snare.

70 days the tent & natron salts
for Thy limbs the linens of Sais

& finally the priest would commence
The Opening of the Mouth the ceremony

to allow the dead to live & speak
when the gates of the Next World opened

ix.
Logo, Logos, Man in Black

The rooster lugs the sun up. Now almost risen,   **crosshatched with stylus**
                                                         clay tablets baked in the sun

◆

so sunspokes flare citron toward a firmament of quarter notes.

◆

                    U   **in use before the spread of**
         S   **N**   **alphabetic writing.**

         ───────────

         record company

◆

Petroglyph, logogram, 45 ascendant in my father's hand

◆

                                         meaning that one written sign
& dropped to the twenty-buck hi-fi where it floats   **represents the entire word**

◆

& wheels, oracling the baritone of Johnny Cash

◆

who is *stuck in Folsom Prison where he can't be free.*

◆   **Sun Single #232,**
                                            released 12/55

O turning wherein word becometh Word, burnished

◆

                                         and there appeared to them
Word, Pentecostal as the lyric flares, molten toward me— **cloven tongues like as of fire**

◆

                                             (Acts 2:2)

there in the basement, blazing mid-air. I can touch

◆

                                         and it sat upon
                                         each of them

with my fingers each winged note & glistening phrase.

◆

I can see. Can see. Those rich folks eating in those

◆

dining cars: fancy suits, ties, the bottles uncorked, the dresses

◆

of the women, are they silken? & I will not be free,

◆

free no more. My father hums along, Jim Beam in his hand

8/26/19–

◆   12/30/90

of course. I am five. Word or flesh? Tell me, tell me.

◆

How shall I travel, Father? Again the needle throbs against the song.

Voyelles: Ring of Fire

(after Rimbaud)

A black, E white, I red, U green, O blue—vowels.

◆

I invented the color of vowels!

How do I conjure your blazing genesis?   **I believed in all enchantments**

◆

A, mother, black: silk elastic garterbelt snap, ink-hiss

◆

as it meets the skin. Flies gone sluggish on a windowsill:

I standardized

the vertigos

November, night lagooning starless. E, pill of smoke in electric train,

◆

funnel-mushroom cloud atop a snowbank, aspirin in Pepsi, flowering.

◆

I, ruby sputum, father: his lost finger & the sabersaw's purling

I wrap it in his

monogrammed handkerchief

crimson spiral, on my knees in sawdust to find the stub, blood-on-the moon.

sewn back ER

17 stitches

U-turn, u-fix-it, u-break-it-u-buy-it. Right Rev. H. Greenlee Hayes

and when He had

given thanks he broke it

semaphoring arms upraised with the Host, glue-alling roof

◆

and gave it to His

of my mouth before the chaliced Blood. Alchemist's stalactite cave,   **Disciples saying**

◆

Bat Cave under Stately Wayne Manor. Cowled Crusader secret identities.

                       ◆

I'll prove that other Self is *Bruce Wayne!* **Get him, men!**

& O pure O—trumpet blare from *Ring of Fire,* where love

                       ◆

is a burnnning thing . . . strangely good, pre-pubescent hard-on

                       ◆   **down down down**

(rubbing church pew in the praying parts), Cherubim, Seraphim,

                       ◆

                                     as the flame came higher

Jericho walls spilt over the plain. Alpha, Omega, my altarboy robe.

xi.

Sangre II: Drink Ye All of This

Black crepe, brass cross, gladiator fishnet—the spray

will snag its glint. I wrap it like Christo,

altarpiece cocooned with bunting, paint it black. Candles

now from the 6th hour
there was darkness

gutter, altar stripped flowerless, organ dead. Good Friday

over all the land

is endless. His agon longer. He's Spartacus

in CinemaScope, writhing stigmatic clots, blood-trails

they gave Him

snaking. Station: He is crowned with thorns. Station: He falls,   vinegar to drink

is nailed. I am bored. Station: for His garment they cast lots.

Bored *senseless*. Reverend Hayes on a roll: "the tremoring nails—

mingled with gall

conjure their pain in your every cell." I squirm,

heavy bored against the pew, sweltering robes. & on he drones.

dizziness aura
first Gran Mal

Then it takes me. The nave careens. White light drills

its spike between my eyes & twitching I am hurled forth,

& behold the veil of the Temple

◆

blind toward Damascus, forehead grazing wood, scarlet plush

◆ **was rent in twain**

against my robe. Head cradled: here begins my newborn life.

◆

the earth did quake.

The Reverend scowls, his pen jabbed down my throat.

Tracking Shot: De Rerum Natura

Point of view: Blackstone top floor ceiling, peering down.

weekend getaway Loop

◆

Ectoplasmic white, their bodies float, coverlet

so too with birds & beasts
both tame & wild

◆

heaved floorward as he enters her, skins phosphorescent

◆

as tablets, bubbling the rim of the glass. Room 731.

superabundance all aglow
their resistance to the generative seed

◆

Dec. '52, pillow beneath her, legs scissoring air,

◆

is quelled by delight
slow strokes first then quick, slow then quick. **by mutual rapture linked**

◆

From both ghostly throats the cries will break.

◆

seeds that course through
As with night-vision glasses, pulsing their infrared blur. **the limbs under the impulse**

◆

I can see but can't see. Picture grainy. See but can't.

of Venus dashed together by
the collusion of mutual passion

Wallet, earring, garter belt. Stockings vaporous on the chair.

◆

of which neither party was
Glint from necklace, gin & tonic flickering by the mirror. **master or mastered**

◆

I am setting out. Salt taste in my mouth, I float.

◆

Seafoam buoyed & the consanguineous cries

◆

which shape me, which shape me, which shape.

composed of atoms

from both sources engendered

◆

radio big band volume low

Venetian blinds, red neon, frozen lake.

◆

Finned cars streak beneath the nimbused lights.

8/22/53–

IV

Can't You Spare Me Over?

(Smithsonian Folkways #40090)

Coal dust webs the lungs & from them slurs the plea.
The banjo notes are nails stabbing pinewood: Dock Boggs
pleading, high and lonesome: *O Death,*

O O Death. Not the archipelagos of Hades.
But surely Stygian water carves the hollows
of Eurydice's bones. *O Death won't you spare me*

over 'til another day. The tape is spooling
on a porch in Lechter, Kentucky. & Death insists,
of course, that we follow standard protocol.

*I bind your feet so you can't walk. I sew
your mouth so you can't talk.* You can feel Him
wet His needle, hover at your lips, stitch & slither

against your jaw, the work as patient
as silicosis. & now a kind of twilight
mists the earth, the strip mine shovels & the company stores,

coal cars rolling the narrow gauge & the barren
Churches of the Nazarene, where not even
bones shall be permitted at The End to rise

& dance & hair from the skulls forever
shall sprout. O Death, give us comfort at least
as the souls drift confounded up & down

the thermals of such mist. In these beds
the I.V. tubes prohibit movement. When I last saw Jake
he tried to pat the nurse's ass, but the chemo drip

was in his way. The request for lemon pie
was bluster & wildly his eyes looked about.
I was elsewhere for the fever which brought

the coma & you know the rest: bedside with my wife,
her mother at vigil in a metal chair & the sodden
April light of Birmingham. Intubated tremble,

machine whirr & the tics & twitches, lips & tongue at work
but silent. *I sew your mouth so you can't talk,*
I bind your legs. For weeks you search the riverbank

for a boat to give you passage. This shape you've taken—
how new & wavering it is, surging like the sawgrass
as it bows to wind & always it is noon, full summer

though nothing warms you & the sleek
dark berries which line these banks are not
for you to taste. They rain upon the ground

beyond your handless reach, never to blue
the creases of your palm, or weave down your beard
to stain your shirt. A kite unmoored, you billow

& those who seek you, reading magazines & thrillers
by your nightstand in their vigil, are figures you can barely glimpse,
waving from the pineys & the milltown smokestacks glinting

from the camelbacked foothills behind you. & forward you inch
but cannot walk & lo you hover on the placid shimmer,
the luminary blues. Everywhere water,

& the jon-boat or trireme you've found
sways oarless in the sun. Peaceful now to drift this way,
the tide lapping slow. You are permitted to remain

as long as you shall require.

(Jake Watson, 1929–1999)

Written on the Due Date of a Son Never Born

Echinacea, bee balm, aster. Trumpet vine
I watch your mother bend to prune, water

sluicing silver from the hose—
                                                    another morning
you will never see. Summer solstice: dragonflies flare

the unpetalled rose. 6 a.m.
                                        & already
she's breaking down, hose flung to the sidewalk

where it snakes & pulses in a steady
keening glitter, both hands to her face. That much

I can give you of these hours.
                                                    That much only.
Fist & blossom forged by salt, trellising

your wounded helixes against our days,
tell us how to live
                                    for we are shades, facing

caged the chastening sun. Our eyes
are scorched & lidless. We cannot bear your light.

Prayer to George Oppen

Below the el stop, barking shepherd, 6-flat
   window and its disembodied arm, watering
a box of herbs.

In my father's herringbone, circa
'62 or 3.
     Alright now to wear it.

Alright to wear it with joy.
   (Dead five years after all.)
   Clarity a moment, then

my train, pneumatic snarl of
   doors and all the music seeping from
the headphoned choir, backward caps

and eyes closed. Car lit bright
   in the overcast day, *a ferocious*
     mumbling, in public

of rootless speech. Clarity a moment,
   then
the scorch mark noticed

on the right sleeve of the jacket.
   How far I am
     even from him, I his *issue.*

And in this motion, from these faces,
     how much farther still?
   This one: awake now, stop missed and

groceries spilled on the aisle,
  adjusting her babushka, scowling.
Instruct me then at least to form

the words. Exact
  the soul house, frayed and woolen.
Pocket, sleeve, faint smell of him.

Pocket, vowel, covenant.

For Townes Van Zandt, 1946–1997

Death was his subject & music & drink his form, & upon him
was bestowed the dubious gift of prophecy—that he would die
at fifty-two, in homage to his father, & on New Year's Day,

in homage to Hank Williams. Death his subject, which is to say
he understood tradition, that life for example, is brutish
& short, but absolved by moments of defining clarity:

rain on a conga drum, the days like rain
on a conga drum. Melodies plaintive & the voice
hurled out from a shaman's cave you visit

when all other means have failed. & you stand
with his ensemble in the winter rain, the outlaws
& chain-smoking whores, the track marks & betrayals,

the dead beloveds forever asleep
on culvert blankets beneath the four-lanes,
the brown bag passed & shared on the curb

with your pals before the heat of the day,
to celebrate your windfall from the sale of plasma.
Our longings are content & content is error.

& our longings are form, which is error as well.
Drink was his form & death was his music,
music his drink & death his form, & a silence

prowls between the notes of his every song,
which is not error, a terrible soothing silence
which tells me, for I love his songs, that the likes

of Townes Van Zandt will never come again, which is
another way to understand tradition,
& another absolving clarity. It was Tucson

but it was snow, Tucson twenty years ago:
half the water pipes in town had burst
& tufts of white fringed the prickly-pears,

saguaros bejewelled with Christmas lights.
& this explains why only six of us had made it
to the club that night. Twelve-string & a back-up band

consisting of a flask upon a stool, some jokes
involving leprechauns, & a chorus which avows
that maybe "she just has to sing

for the sake of the song." Between sets
he sat among us & he talked, mostly to my girlfriend.
Already his face was Audenesque, lines as deep

as his West Texas drawl, head bent down when he spoke.
A double was procured him & by the middle of the second set
his voice was shot, the lyrics slurred & sometimes forgotten

& in the back of the room the desert wind
blew open a door to the parking lot, arcing falsetto
as snow danced the pool tables' felt, the longneck empties

teetering & the chairs already upturned by the men's room door,
corkscrewing white below the beer signs
trembling their neon & the Flashdance

& Farrah posters a-ripple in strict waves. O I & everyone
did not stop breathing, but I tell you no one moved. No one
moved & Townes was elsewhere, gone into where he now

has gone for good: the song lurched on until it was complete.

A Pressure That Makes a Shape as You Go on Describing

It is always wanting more, & failing at that,
desires what it once had: before the second

stroke, for example, when it was a gray
& frantic thing, scrambling from the Rose

of Sharon to the almost shingleless roof
of the empty house on Congress,

where a bucket of tar's been left
against the chimney. & it peers into those depths,

mosquito larvae, fetid rainwater, then slithers
the gutter to a powerline, & so on to another roof,

another. Insistent, several hundred times per minute,
the ventricles hum & it staggers toward

the next room of the wanting or the wanting back.
& it must, in this passage, eat voraciously,

maintaining as well a solemnity, a vigilance,
looking this way & that as it chews & swallows

& the channel selector pulses up & down with
stubborn slowness. It is burnt coffee, track lights,

urine & antiseptic smells & here a sofa
which makes it a lounge, talk show & soap emitting

their snarl & clamor, even as the spoonfed oatmeal
streaks down from between its lips & even as it strives

to express its rage at this turn of events, sounds issued
loudly from the throat—this to indicate, perhaps,

its kinship with the one who feeds it,
who is thinking not of it but of himself,

& hardly of this too-bright common room
where the chair wheels etch black streaks

against linoleum. (Tell me if this is too far for you:
this is not what had been planned.) Not of it

but of himself & of how his woman
last night touched the long jagged seam

across his belly, scar tissue weaving
pale upon the darker goodly flesh,

rib cage down to navel, the line
which makes him flinch where she has touched it,

although his wound was healed years ago.
But she touches it now & is allowed,

strokes it now & is allowed. & the sudden
ease of his permission startles him,

her tongue upon it now, its ridges & its stitchery
brailling upon her fingertips, its each word

slickened with their sweat before she moves down
lower still, parted lips to take him in.

Arion

Hard to roll the wheelchair to poolside,
   & the orderlies, swerving,
      joke with him: how many quads

to unscrew a light bulb? How many
   paras to unhook a bra? That one
      he's heard, & the other one too.

Brakes on now, pool water dimpled,
   salt-tang against his tongue as they
      lower him, device a slapdash hybrid—

net, aluminum chair & canvas straps.
   Above his shoulders, a tingling,
      but the water's mostly *taste*

& memory, coalescing its restless forms:
   Brighton Beach some thirty years gone,
      his able-muscled calves & thighs.

The dolphin spies him first from below,
   legs dangling, though no more
      useless-seeming to her

than any land-born thing's. She circles,
   slower with each rotation,
      & ever-closer, whirlpool & roil,

silvery trireme-prow of dorsal fin,
   beak lathing wave, the blowhole's chuff.
      & then the eyes meeting his,

until it's only the two of them here,
   the orderlies gone, the wet-suited
      keepers with pails of squid.

& he wants, like Arion, to sing.
   So it's Gershwin at first, tentatively hummed,
      & then *Norwegian Wood* & *I've Just*

Seen A Face, so loud his voice—
   she showed me her room . . . —
      is breaking. & now her beak

open to the pink mouth, the jaws'
   tympanic snap—*isn't it good? . . . —*
      blunt teeth, & her cackling

high-pitched harmony—*so I lit*
   a fire . . . —nuzzled beak against
      the salt-rinsed bristle of his beard.

O brine & glossolalic swirl, their eyes
   still locked, the water seething.
      & when I awoke/ I was alone. . . .

Alchemy, Mother Ship, Mile One One Seven

(for Dean Young)

Gnosis isn't possible—not outside Demotte at 6 a.m., big rigs snoring
    in their painted slots,
urinals in half-light made of phosphorus while the hand dryer
    wheezes so two truckers

can argue in privacy the price of crank. Deal made, a grease-shiny hand
    counts twenties, confederate
flag-patch cap bobbing through the door, where I am going too,
    sun rising Heraclitan

fire in this spring of Hale-Bopp, tail billowing just an hour ago
    past Gary. Cusp
of light & dark, middleness stretching endlessly as radio waves.
    Middle of the middle

of the middle. Three days a week our homes are two forty-six
    point seven miles off,
you to the north while I go south, you to the south while I
    go north. Sometimes

on this treeless four-lane I will glimpse your CRX, barrelling Loop-ward
    as the miles tick me closer
instead to the blowzy cornfed children of Muncie & Fort Wayne.
    Middle of the middle:

Logansport, Lebanon, Lafayette, twin Willy Lomans, sample cases
    bulging undergrad sestinas,
Dorm Love 101. So now at last we have our fathers' lives,
    bare-walled rooms for the road,

the salesmen's & railroad men's hotels. (Conjure lamp & chair.
    Conjure dresser with its wallet
& the well-thumbed Gideon, hair-oil smells of 1960, the pillowcase
    Vitalis-drenched.) Accelerate

to 80 & the radio is Dylan screeching *How does it Feeeel . . . ?*
    'BEZ dissembling
to some Jesus Station, dissembling in turn to Heaven's Gate,
    purple shroud & Mother Ship,

websites pulsing their Wormwood Stars, menu of the cult's final meal
    being talk-showed
with Jamesian pedantry. Middle of the middle of the middle:
    & where in this

the Alembic, the Peacock's Tail, Thrice-Great Hermes chanting bone
    to living gold, the lapis-haunted air?
Where the marriage of Sun & Moon, saffron glitter from
    transmuting crucible,

Unconsuming Fyire & where the salamander's flickering tail?
    Gnosis isn't.
We are our fathers' base metal, plummeting 80 down 65, where now
    the element is sleet,

wipers chanting strict iambic though the radio can't scan,
    every station a blaze of static.
& yet this base metal, friend, is dear; is prayer & chosen, & homeless
    & ours. Is radical light

churning west from Ohio, rosy-gloved sunrise rivening its storms—
    precisely at 6:54,
precisely at mile one one seven. Precisely. & the radio coughs,
    reanimating to

a blue-lipped Aussie, frozen to the Everest slope, cell phone
    patched through to his wife
in Brisbane as the blizzard hammers on, talking literally
    to death, last breath beamed

by satellite, *where are we where are we where are we*
    where are we . . .
Static & hiss, hiss & static, rising to The Mother Ship,
    where we're all going too.

But slowly, slowly. & not, my friend, today.

Inscribed on Handmade Paper on the Due Date
of a Daughter Never Born

In tender labor the making began—a robe
flung to the carpet, the candlelight & copious touching,

finger to finger, mouth to mouth, the consummating hope
attested to by sweat & shudder & fashioning

a droplet of original fire.
                              But now you are unmade,
made & unmade daily in our keening

& raw orphanhood: the only means by which your making stays.
Today you are a hundred forty syllables of pain,

impressed into your mother's paper, conjured
from the watermarks of salt, mold & deckle, mottled

poppy blossoms necklacing
                              black letters,
which now make up your body & your shroud.

Winding sheet, cerecloth, cerement, pall. Our making
& unmaking & our labor we bring:
                              a cloak for your crossing.

Choiron

The custom in Athens was to shave it, a practice
thought to be imported from the Persians or the Medes,

shave it smoothly & anoint it with perfumed oils,
so that it glistened when exposed, lamplight dappling

the labial folds; shave it & bejewel it,
scent & shimmer of its maquillage; Thracian ochres,

unguents to redouble its roseate hues,
& complement its heightening tumescence;

shave it to recall some bald, idealized & gracile suavity,
the frankness of prepubescent girls. *Choiros,*

meaning *cunt,* but when it is so lavishly enfetishized,
when it is readied with such ceremony, the proper term

is *Choiron,* the diminutive, applied to emphasize its artful
display—*cuntlet, little cunt, daintiest of figs,*

although an exact translation is impossible,
& those who seek to render it as *pussy,* or *snatch,*

or *twat* or variants thereof, choose to ignore
its more earnest, indeed more hallowed, connotations.

On the Babrinsky Vase in Munich, attributed to Philoneos,
the Hetaera sits with legs spread wide as two companion

Hetaerae kneel with razors at her crotch,
a bowl beside them—soap or oil in which

to dip their instruments. Already the pudendum's nearly hairless.
Foley interprets the scene as rape, citing Foucault:

"the razor's symbolism is of course . . . quite obvious." But shall we
beg to differ? Shall we hymn instead its sleek

& lambent petals? Choiron, how sweetly
do you shine. How shall we praise thy fecund estuaries,

lips to enfold thy altar, nubbed & tremoring,
& salty upon the tongue? Beloved, it has been a year

of sorrow unabated, the dead upon their smoldering pyres
too numerous to reckon, the barrenness, the sleeplessness,

the keening nights exhausted from our petty wars. Saturday afternoon—
you're dozing on the chaise lounge, paperback collapsed

beside you on the carpet, chemise hiked up so that I
may wake you: glottal, umlaut, circle & the tongue extended

full to taste the wettening, saline & wordless tongue,
alembic to nothing but the purest longing & release & the gates

wherein so long we have dwelled in grieving
now shall open. O groan & the consanguineous cries.

Tongue to the door, tongue to the door
& briny with these fluent juices.

Red Ochre

Ozone smell: all afternoon
   the rain turned off and on like spray
      slurring out a tap. She's floating along

the fern bar window, and the couples
   scoring paper tablecloths with crayons,
      circles and arrows as they laugh,

cigarette-glow and darting eyes, margaritas
   all around, salt crust on the glass rims.
      Then she's passed their tinted pane,

sidewalk pocked with drizzle, glazing
   while she kills time, waiting to call
      for the test results. She conjures

the lab, the centrifuges' hiss
   and whirl, specimens and samples
      towering in a room her mind makes

long and narrow as the university
   pool she's walking from, and its air
      as thickly humid. Her sari

billows in the wind and spotty rain.
   She's thinking to think
      away: cedar waxwing, goldfinch,

tarpit, a spike of red ochre
   with one side sharpened—
      a writing stick from Pleistocene

Australia, unearthed in this morning's
   section three. And the fifty-two sons
      of Ramses: someone's cleaning rubble

from all the basalt sarcophagi.
   Think away to her thirty-fourth lap,
      her goggles unfogging and then

the good air swallowed,
   great draughts at the poolside,
      great tectonic draughts.

Chlorine sting, the nostrils
   flaring and her own slick palm
      inching her neck to reckon the pulse.

Recovery Room: Seven Hells

They draw the curtains for the woman has awakened,
thrashing from her lipo. But you're still out,

ashen hand in mine, so much blood loss
the obstetrician told me she was

fearful enough to call for plasma,
& from the twilight of dream & reckoning,

grieving caverns of the world below,
you ask if the child can be shown to you

& held. Shard, delirium, hiss of monitor
& halogen glare, the woman going on

about the way the cuts along her thighs
just ache like bloody hell, until

the Demerol shuts her down. In which
subterranean precinct do you wander now,

shade calling out to shade? Bardo
of the Revenants, Bardo of the Marble

Threshing Floor, Place Where the Hills
Crash Together, Place Where Smoke

Has No Outlet. Or Place
Without the Consolation of a Name. Place

of Antiseptic Smell, numbers a-glow
& twitching on a screen, Place of Tissue

Vacuumed Through a Tube, its wounded
DNA embabeled to a stutter, as though

no different from the yellow lustrations,
globules of fat extracted so as to please

a moaning woman's vanity. Why then
should you wake to this realm? More haunted

than the one in which you dream & call out
& blessedly incorporeal have risen

like smoke to seek the murmurous nothing
that is Lethe. The nurses gather while the woman

wails for a syringe. Sleep now.
Sleep yourself away from this.

Triclinium: Couple Bending to a Burning Photo

Inside ourselves,
inside ourselves so long
       we are engravened there. Inside
   the hot streets mazing
      from the Suq to fractious

cul-de-sacs, piss smell
   & whitewashed alleyways,
      mules & taxi radios throbbing Rai
       & still inside ourselves.
(Still with our own canopic jar—
    pulsing from its negative

    the sonogram, the inkstain heart:
pinprick size & life size both.
     Bitter the book.
   Bitter like vinegar
      the unwritten book.)

Boys with head lice tug our sleeves
    & when with a trowel
      does the site grow laden,
       teetering up & sealed
at last by brick?
   Suddenly the dicey neighborhood,

    Kom al-Shogafa, gives way.
Ticket booth, a caftaned watchman
     sipping tea,
   a single olive tree—off season
      it is permitted

to descend alone. Down
the creaking ladder like Aeneas
& we test each trembling rung,
all to ourselves the shaft,
the fetid water ankle deep,
the walls this far below the June sun

cool to the touch in the edge light
of twenty-watt bulbs,
strung along the switchbacking galleries,
room after catacomb room.
& still inside ourselves.

By rope the dead were pulleyed
down the shaft, slow plummet
of urn, sarcophagi groaning
to rest in stuccoed niches—
Thoth & Isis Hermes Christ,
fish & falcon eye

blinking open to our flashlight,
Anubis in bas-relief
in armor of a Roman legionnaire.
*A confusion of styles
and religious traditions.*

Capital with sacred bull,
seated water-streaked baboon,
room upon room
inside ourselves,
caduceus seething blue vipers.
Dead end & gallery & on her knees

N. peers haloed in the bulb's
burnished shimmer, stroking cool stone,

a niche for a child,
barely the length of her arm.
& now before us the famed

vaulted room, dome soaring up
as the lights begin to flicker,
blinking twice & off.
Darkness so thick we breathe it.
Then N. with flashlight
rummaging her backpack

for the grapes & cheese,
baguette & tannic
Sinai merlot
("Omar Khayyam Red"),
her jackknife glinting in the beam.

All this way. All this way
to mourn again our child in a room
of couches hewn from living rock.
Triclinium—
"the place of banquet
for remembrance of the dead."

Far-off drip of cistern water
& to the stone we pour
the first libation,
the black wine hissing out.
O spirit beyond hunger,

we set down to you such offerings
as will appease thee, body
unborn of our bodies,
bread of our bread.
O circle within circle, imprinted gray

on the sonogram's firmament,
crosses & arrows glyphed
across thee to map thy size.
We strike the lighter & we lay your photo
on the ancient threshing floor of souls.

& only for an instant do you flare.

Kill Born, Weed Smoke, Chk Mark, Onchola Senn

The two officers say they will appeal.
     The kid, one Jeremiah Mearday, says he was just
  on his way to the drugstore

    for some cold meds. The cops say
     they didn't even have with them
  the flashlights said to have been used

      to break his jaw, & extract four teeth,

one of which was swallowed. He fell
     "accidentally" while resisting arrest.
  They decline to explain the blood

    later found on both the flashlight handles,
     neither of which, anyway,
  "were in their possession at the time."

      Don't misconstrue: Jeremiah Mearday

is likely a wicked little shit, on his way
     on the night in question to score some crack.
  & it happened that for whatever reasons

    he had gone outside unarmed.
     The cops' attorneys natter from the radio
  while the March snow takes its time

     in melting & all winter I've looked out

on a skein of cassette tape tangled in
        the branches of my window's elm,
    glinting tinsel when the sun attempts

        to strike it: O poor self named me, etc.
            150 mg. of regulation daily: the new pill's
    pentagonal-shaped & hefty,

        a "W" incised on its side, an upturned

Monopoly house. (O Zoloft Avenue,
        Effexor Gardens, Wellbutrin Railroad
    chugging to Paxil Place.) N.'s again unpregnant,

        & medicates herself downstairs
            on murder mysteries, but now she's
    at my desk to announce some Senn High Homeboys

        are back to tag our garage again,

"right there in goddamn daylight." Out the window
        you can see a crouching form,
    spraying out Sumerian for the third time

        since Christmas. KILL BORN WEED SMOKE
            CHK MARK—spondees are the rage
    this year. DEATH ANG favors red, though sometimes

        classic black & I'm throwing on my overcoat,

while N. calls the cops, who I hope will not arrive
        with flashlights, if they ever arrive.
    & all afternoon I'll bathe the garage

with acetone-stinking brushes & rags. O Onchola Senn,
    the palace of learning which sports your name
fuses the architectural traditions

    of the Parthenon & Leavenworth;

Doric columns loom within a twenty-two foot
    chain-link fence, metal detectors buzzing
at the doors. Look you now upon these

    glyphs & symbols, circles, arrows, labyrinths.
       & when I reach the garage I see the taggers
are in fact a crouching boy

       & a seated girl who won't stop weeping

into the boy's cupped hands. "Easy baby,
    easy baby. Look at me I'm here with you."
Hands ungloved & circling now

    her forehead & her cheeks. Easy baby
in the mud-flecked snow beside
the car lot dumpster & the neighbor's heaved-out

    dresser, gaping drawerless as he ministers

& she's almost quieted as I reach them & glaring he turns
    without pausing the swirl & laving
rhythms of his hands. "It ain't your business, man" & then

    again it's easy baby; it is circle, glyph
       & labyrinth & proffered mercies tendered with
wingbeat, the stylus-tip of finger-pressure, o not

    my business anyway & easy baby, easy baby easy.

Notes

Many thanks to Bill Olsen, Nancy Eimers, David Jauss, Tony Whedon, Dean Young, Roger Mitchell, and Brian Teare. And ongoing gratitude to Ed Ochester.

"To the Memory of Paul Celan": See Lucette Matalon Lagnado and Sheila Cohn Dekel's *Children of the Flames: Dr. Josef Mengele and the Untold Story of the Twins of Auschwitz;* Port Arthur, Tasmania, was Australia's most notorious penal colony.

"Symposium": *in the naked bed, in Plato's cave*—sampled from a poem by Delmore Schwartz.

"Zola the Hobbyist": Zola was an avid amateur photographer. The final couplet is a verbatim quotation, drawn from Beaumont Newhall's *The History of Photography.*

"And the Unclean Spirits . . .": "For he said unto him, 'Come out of the man, thou unclean spirit.' And he asked him, 'What is thy name?' And he answered saying, 'My name is Legion, for we are many.'" After a bit of bargaining, Christ persuades the evil spirits—"they were about two thousand"—to leave the madman and inhabit a herd of swine, who then hurl themselves off a cliff to drown in the sea: much has been made of this puzzling incident. (In truth, pigs are excellent swimmers.)

"Testings, 1956": The TV quiz show scandals of the 1950s. "Luciferon" is the name of the substance which enables fireflies to blink. The poem owes a debt to Cynthia Huntington.

"Stalin's Library Card": The interrogations of Mandelstam and Babel are reported in Vitaly Shentalinsky's *The KGB's Literary Archive.* Section VII owes a debt to David King's *The Commissar Vanishes: The Falsification of Photographs and Art in Stalin's Russia.* Special thanks to Phil Metres and Noelle Watson for their bibliographical skills.

"Tribulation Eclogue": See Richard Hough's *Captain James Cook: A Biography.* The Asian Spotted Longhorn Beetle infestation was first discovered in Cook County in 1998; the insects probably came from air freight sent from Southeast Asia to O'Hare. Australia had a bizarre fixation with the Simpson trial.

"The Art of Poetry": Based on various accounts of Shackleton's benighted trans-Antarctic expedition, especially Alfred Lansing's *Endurance: Shackleton's Incredible Voyage.*

"Word Horde against the Gnostics": See James M. Robinson's *The Nag Hammadi Library.* Also, "Sam Cooke and the Soul Stirrers: The Specialty Years." The Ramones' version of "Needles and Pins" originally appeared on "Road To Ruin."

"After Propertius" takes as its model W. G. Shepherd's version of Propertius, Book IV.7. Robert Lowell's version of the same poem, included in *Lord Weary's Castle,* was also in the back of my mind.

"For the Centenary of Hart Crane": By the time of Crane's suicide in 1933, his mother was more or less destitute. A dedicated spiritualist, she believed that her son's "posthumous" poems, dictated via a psychic during séances, would eventually be published and bring her some much-needed income.

"Dirge with Proofs" alludes to the Oklahoma City bombing of April 1995.

"Spirit Cabinet": See Eugene Taylor's *Shadow Culture: Psychology and Spirituality in America:* "Shakers were always known for their trance worship and alleged psychic abilities. Still on display in the Harvard Society is a spirit cabinet, in front of which believers would sit, waiting for a communication from beyond."

"Crayola": a partial list of the rubrics and samples—Emanuel Swedenborg, *Heaven and Hell; Children's Golden Illustrated Bible; Hoyle's Book of Games;* Edward Shorter, *A History of Psychiatry; Flash Comics* (#132); The Tokens, "The Lion Sleeps Tonight"; T. S. Eliot, "The Wasteland" (290–310); Plato, *The Symposium;* Robert Drews, *The End of the Bronze Age;* Peter Gay, *The Cultivation of Hatred;* Samuel Taylor Coleridge, "Kubla Khan"; Nigel A. Fox, *A Boy's Book of Alexander;* Jared Diamond, *Guns, Germs and Steel;* Celeste Olalquiga, *The Artificial Kingdom: A Treasury of the Kitsch Experience; The Egyptian Book of the Dead;* Johnny Cash, "The Sun Years"; The Book of Acts; Arthur Rimbaud, "Vowels"; *Detective Comics* (#303); Cesar Vallejo, *The Complete Posthumous Poetry;* Lucretius, *On the Nature of Things;* Robert Lowell, "For the Union Dead."

"Can't You Spare Me Over?": Dock Boggs's version of "O Death" appears on his "The Complete Folkways Recordings."

"For Townes Van Zandt, 1946–1997": most of the lyrics quoted come from a live recording, "Rear View Mirror."

"Alchemy, Mother Ship, Mile One One Seven" makes reference to the 1997 mass suicide of the Heaven's Gate Cult, and the mountaineer deaths on Everest of the same year.

"Choiron": See James Davidson's *Courtesans and Fishcakes: The Consuming Passions of Classical Athens.*

"Recovery Room": The Aztecs believed in seven hells; see David Carrasco's *City of Sacrifice: The Aztec Empire and the Role of Violence in Civilization.*

"Triclinium: Couple Bending to a Burning Photo": Alexandria, the catacombs.

"Kill Born, Weed Smoke, Chk Mark, Onchola Senn": A neo-classical high school building on Chicago's far north side named for Polish-American educator Nicholas Senn.

Acknowledgments

Acknowledgment is made to the following publications where these poems first appeared, sometimes in earlier versions:

The New Breadloaf Anthology of Contemporary American Poetry: "After Propertius" and "Word Horde against the Gnostics"; *Boulevard*: "Recovery Room: Seven Hells"; *Colorado Review*: "Prayer to George Oppen"; *Crab Orchard Review*: "For Townes Van Zandt, 1946–1997"; *Crazyhorse*: "After Propertius" and "For the Centenary of Hart Crane"; *Denver Quarterly*: "With Divers Illustrations," "Marvel, Eschatology, Transistor," "Rime of the New Types of Weaponry," and "Voyelles" (all from "Crayola"); *5 AM*: "And the Unclean Spirits Went Out of the Man, and Entered into Swine"; *Green Mountains Review*: "Choiron"; *Harvard Review*: "Testings, 1956"; *Hayden's Ferry Review*: "Alchemy, Mother Ship, Mile One One Seven"; *Kenyon Review*: "Cartouche" and "Kill Born, Weed Smoke, Chk Mark, Onchola Senn"; *Michigan Quarterly Review*: "Spirit Cabinet"; *New England Review*: "Poison, 1959"; *Paris Review*: "Days of 1994"; *Ploughshares*: "Red Ochre" and "Triclinium: Couple Bending to a Burning Photo"; *Poetry*: "Arion," "Stalin's Library Card," and "Zola the Hobbyist: 1895"; *Quarterly West*: "Inscribed on Handmade Paper on the Due Date of a Daughter Never Born," "To Hermes Are Attributed Three Inventions," and "To the Memory of Paul Celan"; *Shenandoah*: "Tribulation Eclogue" and "Written on the Due Date of a Son Never Born"; *The Southern Review*: "The Ravenswood"; *Third Coast*: "Dirge with Proofs," "Firstborn of Egypt," and "Word Horde against the Gnostics"; *TriQuarterly*: "'Asend the Stare: On Top Floor Please Ring Bell,'" "Can't You Spare Me Over?" and "The Art of Poetry"; *Volt*: "Tiresias & Crayola," "First Death in Minnesota," "Logo, Logos, Man in Black," "Sangre II: Drink Ye All of This," and "Tracking Shot: De Rerum Natura" (all from "Crayola").

I am grateful to the Illinois Arts Council for a grant which gave me time to write some of these poems.

DAVID WOJAHN is the author of five previous volumes of poetry. *Icehouse Lights,* his first collection, was selected by Richard Hugo as a winner of the Yale Younger Poets Award for 1981, and also received the Poetry Society of America's William Carlos Williams Book Award. His subsequent collections, all published in the Pitt Poetry Series, are *Glassworks* (1987), *Mystery Train* (1990), *Late Empire* (1994), and *The Falling Hour* (1997). He has also published a volume of essays on contemporary poetry, *Strange Good Fortune* (2001), and edited *The Only World* (1995), a posthumous collection of Lynda Hull's poetry. He has received fellowships from the National Endowment for the Arts, the Fine Arts Work Center in Provincetown, and the Illinois and Indiana Councils for the Arts; as well as the George Kent Memorial Prize from *Poetry* magazine and the Amy Lowell Traveling Poetry Scholarship. He has taught creative writing and literature at a number of universities, including the University of Chicago, the University of Houston, and the University of Alabama. He is presently professor of English and director of the Creative Writing Program at Indiana University, and a member of the faculty of the M.F.A. in Writing Program at Vermont College.